FA

Turk

DAN J. MARLOWE

GLOBE FEARON
Pearson Learning Group

FASTBACK® SPORTS BOOKS

Cover Comstock Images. All photography © Pearson Education, Inc. (PEI) unless specifically noted.

ISBN 0-13-024609-3
Printed in the United States of America
1 2 3 4 5 6 7 8 9 10   07 06 05 04 03

Globe
Fearon
Pearson Learning Group

1-800-321-3106
www.pearsonlearning.com

When the Hawk-eyes' shot rebounded from our basket and the ball came directly to Sam, I jumped up from my seat on the bench. The miss had kept the score still tied. Sam whipped a half-court pass to Phil Sheridan, who had half a step on his man. "Go, Phil, go!" I screamed. Nobody ran Phil down from behind on a basketball court.

And then everyone stopped running. The referee was waving off the play. Coach Reardon had called a time-out. I couldn't believe it. With Phil all but free to score the winning basket, coach Reardon had called time-out. I turned to Ron Elliott standing beside me. "I guess the coach didn't get enough TV time yet," I said.

Elliott heard me. Since the crowd had hushed when they realized what had happened, the whole bench heard me, too, including the coach. His face turned red. Elliott turned away from me, and shook his head.

I looked up at the clock. Nine seconds left. Sure, we could set up a play and have a good chance of making it work. But if the coach hadn't called time, Phil would have had a better chance. I moved out of the way, so the five guys coming over to the bench would have room to kneel down around the coach.

"Williams!" Coach Reardon snapped at me. "Go in for Breed! You inbound the ball!"

I couldn't believe it. I looked down the bench to where Dr. Corell always sat. His seat was empty. Where could Doc be at a moment like this? I hesitated. Doc hadn't given me the OK to test my stress-fractured foot under game conditions yet. I'd only been practicing at about three-quarter speed during the week.

But then it hit me. Here was a chance to play. And play when it counted. I saw Tommy Breed moving away from the starting lineup. I knelt down in his place. My guard partner when I was playing, Sonny Barcelona, nudged me in the ribs. "Let's do it, Turk," he muttered.

I watched coach Reardon diagram the

play he wanted. Inbounds from me to Sam Jordan, then back to me when I stepped onto the court. I was to look for Bob Fields cutting to the basket and get the ball to him. The second choice was to get it to Sam, our senior forward.

We went out onto the floor. I checked in at the scorer's table and settled myself at mid court, out-of-bounds. The ref was standing four feet away, holding the ball. A jumping jack in a Hawkeye jersey was bounding up and down in front of me, waving his arms, even before the play started.

The ref tossed me the ball. I had timed the jumping jack. When he was on his way down from a jump, I passed the ball to Sonny, who was sprinting toward me. My man turned away, and Sonny got the ball back to me the second I stepped onto the floor. I looked downcourt. Bob Fields was where I expected him to be. He was running slowly, just about inside his opponent's jersey.

Fields would get you 15 to 20 points, any time you didn't need them. When the crunch came, you couldn't find him. He didn't want the ball then. And he made sure he didn't get it. Everyone on the team knew it, except coach Reardon.

Since I was expecting it, it was no problem. Sam Jordan was cutting toward the basket from the right. I zipped the ball to him. Then I started toward the hoop from the left, running hard, not even thinking about my foot. Sam pulled up, faked a jump shot, shed his man, and popped his shot into the air.

All the bodies were on the other side of the basket. I had a clear lane. Sam's shot looked long. I jumped. I was a foot above the basket when the rebound came off the glass. I hardly had to reach at all. I didn't try to catch it. I slapped it down through the basket with my left hand.

The gym exploded. The guys mobbed me. "Hey, Turk! Hey, Turk!" they were all yelling. The Hawkeyes didn't even think of trying to call a time-out. The game ended. State U. had won a game it wasn't supposed to. One more and we'd be in the play-offs.

Everyone cheered as we ran off the court. I was laughing as we walked down the runway to the dressing room. I couldn't help it. I hadn't even thought I'd get to play. Now the headline would read "STATE SOPHOMORE SINKS WINNING BASKET." I couldn't wait to see Cheryl.

But first I saw Dr. Corell. He came dashing up to me, his face as red as Reardon's had been on the bench. "Who gave you the OK to play?" he shouted. "That foot—who said to try it in a game?"

"Hey, Doc," I protested. "You know who sends the players out onto the floor here."

Silently, he wheeled around and trotted over to Reardon. I could see him bugging Reardon about it, and I could hear Reardon's answer. "Buddy thought he heard you say Williams was ready to play," the coach said easily.

"Buddy" was Buddy Canton, our assistant coach. Doc Corell threw his arms up into the air and walked away. He came back and caught me when I was dressed and ready to leave. "You come to my office in the morning," he ordered. "I want to examine that foot again."

"Sure, Doc," I agreed.

I went out into the runway. Cheryl Hunter was leaning against the opposite wall. She's the Number One player on the women's basketball team. She's not my girlfriend, but I'd like her to be. She's a senior, and a lot of the time she thinks of me as a kid. She never says so, though. And she knows the game and can play it. She's a demon at driving to the hoop. We pay a lot of one-on-one in the gym, and I have the bruises to prove it.

"Well, hero," she greeted me. "How in the world did you ever get into the game? The way coach Reardon feels about your fast-running mouth even when you're healthy, I never expected to see it."

"Neither did I," I admitted. "Maybe he was giving me a chance to fall on my face, putting me in cold?"

"I wouldn't go that far," Cheryl said. "Although he had a tie game. The worst he was going to get was overtime. I wonder."

Cheryl didn't like Reardon any better than I did. I took her arm and we started out for post-game hamburgers. "He hasn't liked you since the first week of practice, in your freshman year," she continued.

That was when I'd made my mark on Coach Reardon. He liked to practice with the players the first couple of weeks, before they really got into shape. We'd been playing three-on-three, with him guarding me. I'd had to inbound a pass, almost like in tonight's game. Reardon was crowding me even more than the guy tonight.

"Pass the ball! Pass the ball!" he kept yelling, right in my face. I tried to move him back and he wouldn't move. So I slammed the ball right off his foot. It came back to me and I picked it up and made the inbound pass. It left Reardon on the floor holding his foot, trying not to show he was in pain. Reardon was wrong, and I was wrong, but there it was. I had nobody crowding me on inbound passes after that.

It had cost me, though. I'd come to

State U. as a forward. A week later Reardon told me I was a guard. He had decided that Bob Fields was going to play the forward spot I had already marked off as mine. I must have spent a thousand hours in the gym learning to play guard.

It's funny how things work out. I'd been a medium-sized forward at six feet five inches. That height made me a big guard. By sophomore year, I'd become the point guard, running the team. And I could always shoot. Reardon had done me a favor without either of us realizing it. But then halfway through the season, I'd gotten hurt, and it was nothing but bench time after that.

I told Cheryl that I would be seeing Doc Corell in the morning. "I hope he lets me play on Saturday," I said.

"What makes you think Reardon would play you even if Doc okayed it, Turk? I don't think Reardon feels it's necessary to make you a star."

"Don't be so cheerful," I told her.

The next morning, I met Doc Corell at his office. He examined the foot and took X-rays again. He kept grunting to himself while he studied the slides against a strong light. "Much better," he said finally. "It's healed very well."

"Does that mean I can play Saturday, Doc?"

He hesitated. "All right," he said finally. "But only for short periods of time."

"Great!" I said. "Thanks, Doc."

Coach Reardon's office was just down the hallway from the doctor's. I knocked once on his door and opened it. Reardon was sitting at his desk with Sandy Martin, the sports editor from the local newspaper.

"Excuse me," I apologized. "Coach, I just wanted to let you know that Doc says I can play on Saturday."

"You're not in shape, Williams," Reardon replied.

"You mean you won't play him after what he did for you last night?" Martin spoke up. He was grinning at me.

"Oh, if the flow of the game calls for it,

I will . . . ," Reardon said, his voice trailing off. He was always worried about newspaper criticism. Any kind of criticism. Which was why I had never been very high on his list of favorites.

I waved to Martin and went down the hall. Passing the gym, I heard the thump-thump-thump of a basketball. I knew who it was, even before I opened the door. Sonny Barcelona was dribbling and shooting baskets between classes.

"Hey, man!" he greeted me. "You really showed Reardon up last night. The guys thought it was great."

"You think I was supposed to blow it?"

"He sure didn't think you were going to win it." Sonny had been smiling, but then he turned serious. "Say, did you hear that Fields is showing a junior college hotshot around campus? He's putting him up over the weekend."

"Why? Reardon doesn't have any scholarships to give next year, even to the best junior college player in the country. He's used up his quota."

"Suppose he took back one of his current scholarships?"

"Hey, Sonny, you're not exactly making my day. Have you heard anything?"

"No, but why else is the guy here? Reardon would love to bring in someone to make Fields look good. Make Reardon look good, too."

"Instead of showing him up like I do? Yeah, I see what you mean. Me and my big mouth. He's such a big fat target, though. I just can't help letting air out of his balloon."

"Want to shoot around?" Sonny asked, offering me the ball.

"No, thanks. See you later."

I had an hour until my Spanish class started.

I crossed the campus to Cheryl's dormitory. I needed some advice. She had a head on her shoulders. All I seemed to have was a mouth.

Cheryl was in the lounge, reading. She put down her textbook when I came in. "Trouble?" she asked right away. She doesn't have much difficulty reading the looks on my face.

I explained to her about the hotshot on

campus as a possible transfer, plus Reardon just about telling me I wasn't going to play Saturday night. "Do you think I'm paranoid to feel Reardon could be loading up the toe of his boot for me, Cheryl?"

"No," she said thoughtfully. "No, I don't. In view of the manner in which you go out of your way to annoy him."

"He invites it, Cheryl. Personality aside, he's not even a good coach."

"But you need him if you're serious about getting your degree."

"You bet I'm serious. I'll never make it in the pros. I'd like to be a starter here, but I don't have any crazy dreams about a pro career."

"Then you've got to convince Reardon he needs you. Or that he'd run into too much trouble trying to get rid of you.

Knowing him, that would probably work better. What's involved in pulling a scholarship?"

"Well, it's seldom done outright. If he's planning it, Reardon probably feels he could get away with it by saying my injury makes me too much of a risk for next year. But it's not like they say, 'You're fired.' Instead they set up four or five hundred circumstances, all nasty, to make you quit. Pile things up on you until you quit."

"Couldn't you sit tight and outlast him?"

"I've seen guys try it. It doesn't work. They turn things around so that even your own teammates feel you're hurting the team by not moving on. They can really put pressure on you."

"And with your famous temper. . . ."
Cheryl was tapping a pencil against her
teeth. "We've got to think this through.
You know, Turk, you've got yourself to
blame for a lot of this."

"A nice guy like me?"

She ticked off her fingers one after
another. "As an athlete, you're arrogant
and you have a bit of a mean streak.
Which isn't all bad. But as a human being
Turk . . ."

"Being modest doesn't become me,
Cheryl."

"It's going to have to become you if
you're planning to stay in school. Or
you're going to need enough leverage
. . . ," she paused, with her pencil tapping
again. "Let me think about it," she said.

I went on to my Spanish class.

When I got back to my room in the athletic dorm, there was a note for me to stop in at assistant coach Buddy Canton's office. I looked at it with a chill feeling in my stomach. Could they really do this to me?

I telephoned Cheryl.

I sat across from Buddy Canton's desk, watching him give me the evil eye. He wasted no time. "We don't think you can cut it any more, Williams," he laid it on the line.

"You're wrong," I told him. *Don't say*

too much, Cheryl had warned me. *Just enough to make your points.*

"Plus your attitude is bad," Canton continued. I didn't say anything. "And that spoils the team's attitude."

"I don't happen to think so."

"We think you're . . ."

"What about my scholarship?" I cut him off.

Canton shrugged. "You wouldn't want to stick the school for a free ride, would you?"

"Are you saying I'm physically unable to play?"

Cheryl had said they were too smart to make any flat statements. "We're saying that for the good of the team . . . ," Canton began.

"I'm staying, Canton," I said, cutting him off again. "For all four years." I could see Canton was puzzled. Based on past performances, he had probably expected me to go over the desk after him. And if it hadn't been for Cheryl, I probably would have. That would have given them all the reason they needed to dump me.

He turned as red as a soft tomato. "We're saying that you won't enjoy it," he said, stiffly.

"Are you speaking of harassment? Lack of playing time?"

"We're saying you won't enjoy it," he repeated.

I got tired of it. I reached across his desk and pulled his phone toward myself. Then I dialed Sandy Martin's number at the newspaper, which I had printed on my palm just before entering Canton's office. "Hi, Sandy," I said to the sportswriter, when he came on the line. "This is Turk Williams."

"Hi, Turk," he responded. "What's up?"

"I'm holding a press conference Saturday night after the game, Sandy," I said. "I hope you'll be there. It has to do with the basketball program here at State U. I think you'll find it interesting," I finished, with a smile at Canton.

"What's the main thrust going to be?"

"No hints. Except you could call it a view from inside."

"Wouldn't miss it," he said. "I'll spread the word around."

"Thanks," I said, and hung up the

phone. I shoved it back across the desk. "Tell Coach Reardon he's invited. You, too."

Buddy Canton was about to explode. "Do you think a jerk kid like you can blackmail us?" he demanded angrily.

"Not if you don't mind the truth coming out about the way you two run the program," I said.

"You'll never play basketball here or anywhere else!" he threatened.

Despite Cheryl's warning, I lost my temper. "If I don't play, you won't coach," I promised him. "I'm not going to roll over and play dead for you."

I got up and walked toward the door. "Don't forget to shave Saturday night," I needled him, on my way out. "There'll probably be some guys there covering it for TV."

I started Saturday night's game. Reardon had caved in, just as I'd known he would. I couldn't breathe after five minutes, and had to take myself out of the game. Reardon looked happy. But I gave him the eye when my throat and chest loosened up, and he put me back in. After that it was all right.

The guys were doing everything they could to make me look good. Sam Jordan and Phil Sheridan were cutting for the basket all night. I'd drive to the hoop, then dish it off, and they'd go up and score. They scored so often that they ran up my assist total. With three baskets by Sonny, from long range after passes from me, my assists at the half numbered thirteen. It wasn't an unlucky number.

Cheryl had brought along half of the girls from her sorority house. Every time I touched the ball, they cheered. They got the crowd into it, too. After a while, all I had to do was scratch my nose and I was cheered.

What could have been a tough game turned into a laugher. The easy win put us into the conference tournament. That meant I'd get to play at least three more games even if we didn't win it. Enough to prove to everyone that I could play. I even made half a dozen baskets myself, as if to emphasize the point.

We hadn't discussed it, but it was understood that if I played, I wouldn't blow the whistle about the program. Still, Reardon looked nervous when we reached the dressing room and saw the reporters and the cameras.

"Clothes on, guys," I told the team. "We're going to have women among us."

Cheryl led some of her gang into the room. The photographers were surprised. Then, they figured they had better start snapping pictures of the young women. This was Cheryl's idea, too. "If you play, and you can't blast Reardon and Canton, you'll still need something for the press conference," she had pointed out.

27

I introduced her to the press, and she took over. Her sorority, Kappa Pi Alpha, was setting up a program to tutor student-athletes who needed it, she announced. It would be an ongoing and open-ended program. And it would result in a greater number of athletes getting enough credits to graduate.

There was polite applause.

It wasn't what the assembled press had expected.

"And it's at Coach Reardon's suggestion that this program is being started," Cheryl added.

Reardon looked startled, but then beamed and aimed his best profile at the cameras.

I could never have brought myself to say that last part, but Cheryl's a politi-

cian. "You go along to get along," she'd
told me. "It's time you grew up."

So I guess I'm growing up.

I couldn't truthfully say I'd become
humble. But after what I'd just been
through, I'll guarantee I was less arrogant
than before.

You never appreciate what you have
until you're faced with losing it.